SCIENCE BEHIND THE COLORS
FLAMINGOS

by Alicia Z. Klepeis

pogo

Ideas for Parents and Teachers

Pogo Books let children practice reading informational text while introducing them to nonfiction features such as headings, labels, sidebars, maps, and diagrams, as well as a table of contents, glossary, and index.

Carefully leveled text with a strong photo match offers early fluent readers the support they need to succeed.

Before Reading

- "Walk" through the book and point out the various nonfiction features. Ask the student what purpose each feature serves.
- Look at the glossary together. Read and discuss the words.

Read the Book

- Have the child read the book independently.
- Invite him or her to list questions that arise from reading.

After Reading

- Discuss the child's questions. Talk about how he or she might find answers to those questions.
- Prompt the child to think more. Ask: What flamingos eat determines their coloring. Do you know of any other animals that change color based on their diet?

Pogo Books are published by Jump!
5357 Penn Avenue South
Minneapolis, MN 55419
www.jumplibrary.com

Copyright © 2021 Jump!
International copyright reserved in all countries.
No part of this book may be reproduced in any form without written permission from the publisher.

Library of Congress Cataloging-in-Publication Data

Names: Klepeis, Alicia, 1971- author.
Title: Flamingos / by Alicia Z. Klepeis.
Description: Pogo books edition.
Minneapolis, MN: Jump!, Inc., 2021.
Series: Science behind the colors | Includes index.
Audience: Ages 7-10 | Audience: Grades 2-3
Identifiers: LCCN 2020000328 (print)
LCCN 2020000329 (ebook)
ISBN 9781645275800 (hardcover)
ISBN 9781645275817 (paperback)
ISBN 9781645275824 (ebook)
Subjects: LCSH: Flamingos–Juvenile literature.
Classification: LCC QL696.C56 K54 2021 (print)
LCC QL696.C56 (ebook) | DDC 598.3/5–dc23
LC record available at https://lccn.loc.gov/2020000328
LC ebook record available at https://lccn.loc.gov/2020000329

Editor: Jenna Gleisner
Designer: Molly Ballanger

Photo Credits: pandapaw/Shutterstock, cover; Reinhold Leitner/Shutterstock, 1; Sanit Fuangnakhon/Shutterstock, 3, 23; cyo bo/Shutterstock, 4; GUDKOV ANDREY/Shutterstock, 5; Christopher Bies/Dreamstime, 6-7; muratart/Shutterstock, 8-9; Alexandre Laprise/Shutterstock, 10; TheRocky41/Shutterstock, 11; Napat/Shutterstock, 12-13; Oleksii Humeniuk/Shutterstock, 14-15; Evelyn D. Harrison/Shutterstock, 16; Steve Gettle/Minden Pictures/SuperStock, 17; Nolleks86/Shutterstock, 18-19; NHPA/SuperStock, 20-21.

Printed in the United States of America at Corporate Graphics in North Mankato, Minnesota.

For Mayim, the coolest flamingal.

3 5944 00147 1422

TABLE OF CONTENTS

CHAPTER 1
Fantastic Flocks 4

CHAPTER 2
Pink Feathers 10

CHAPTER 3
Pink Dancers 16

ACTIVITIES & TOOLS
Try This! 22
Glossary 23
Index 24
To Learn More 24

CHAPTER 1
FANTASTIC FLOCKS

What birds have bright pink feathers and sleep standing on one leg? These fantastic fliers are flamingos!

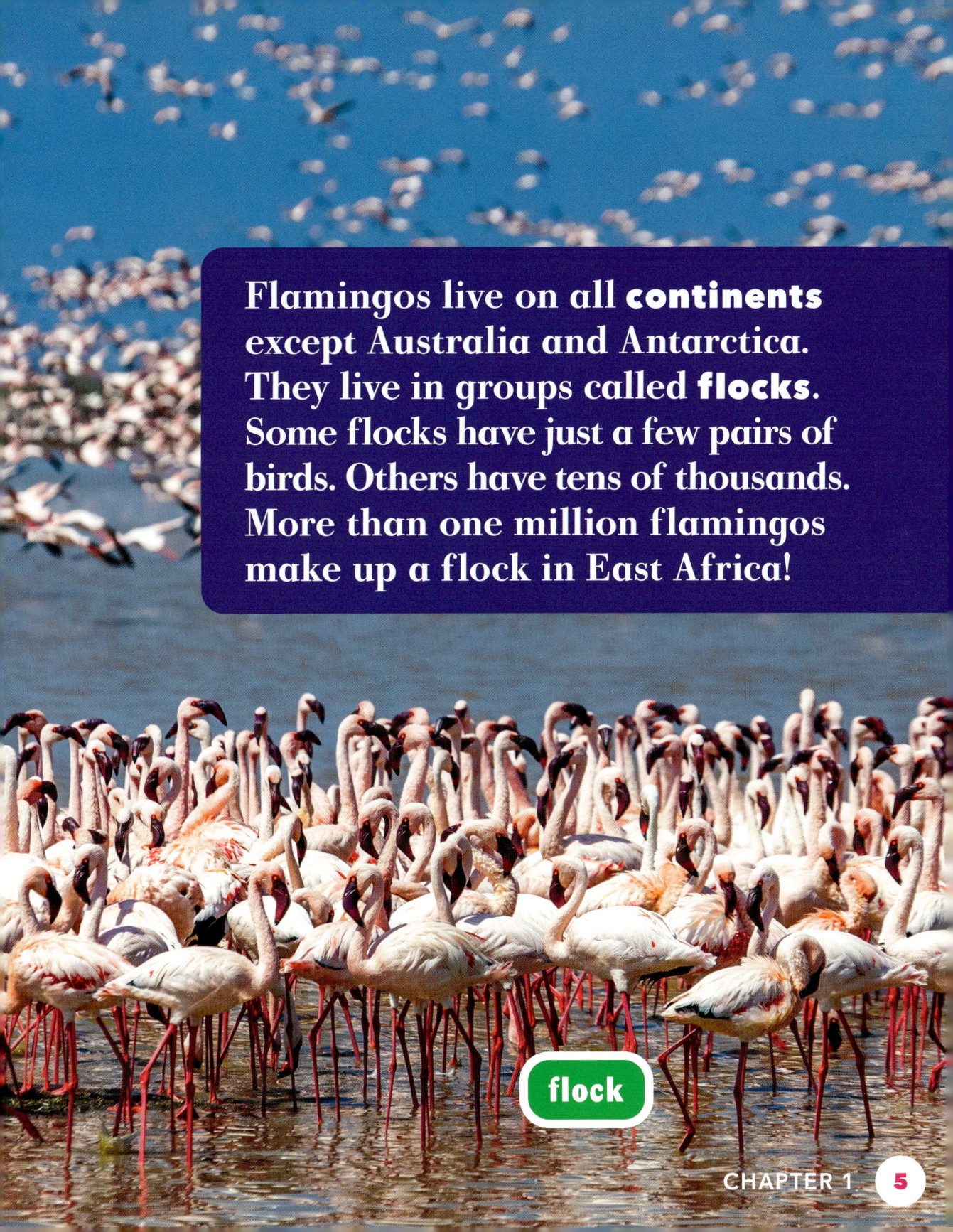

Flamingos live on all **continents** except Australia and Antarctica. They live in groups called **flocks**. Some flocks have just a few pairs of birds. Others have tens of thousands. More than one million flamingos make up a flock in East Africa!

flock

Flocks do just about everything together. This includes sleeping at the same time. Flamingos have long, thin legs. They sleep standing on just one leg. Why? It takes less **energy**. The birds have perfect balance. What if it is windy? They just sway while they sleep!

DID YOU KNOW?

Flamingos have long necks. They often rest their heads on their bodies while they sleep. This helps their neck muscles rest.

leg

CHAPTER 1   7

Webbing between their toes helps them "run" over water. Why do they do this? They run to gain speed. Then they take to the sky!

CHAPTER 1

TAKE A LOOK!

The webbing between their three toes helps flamingos balance. Take a look!

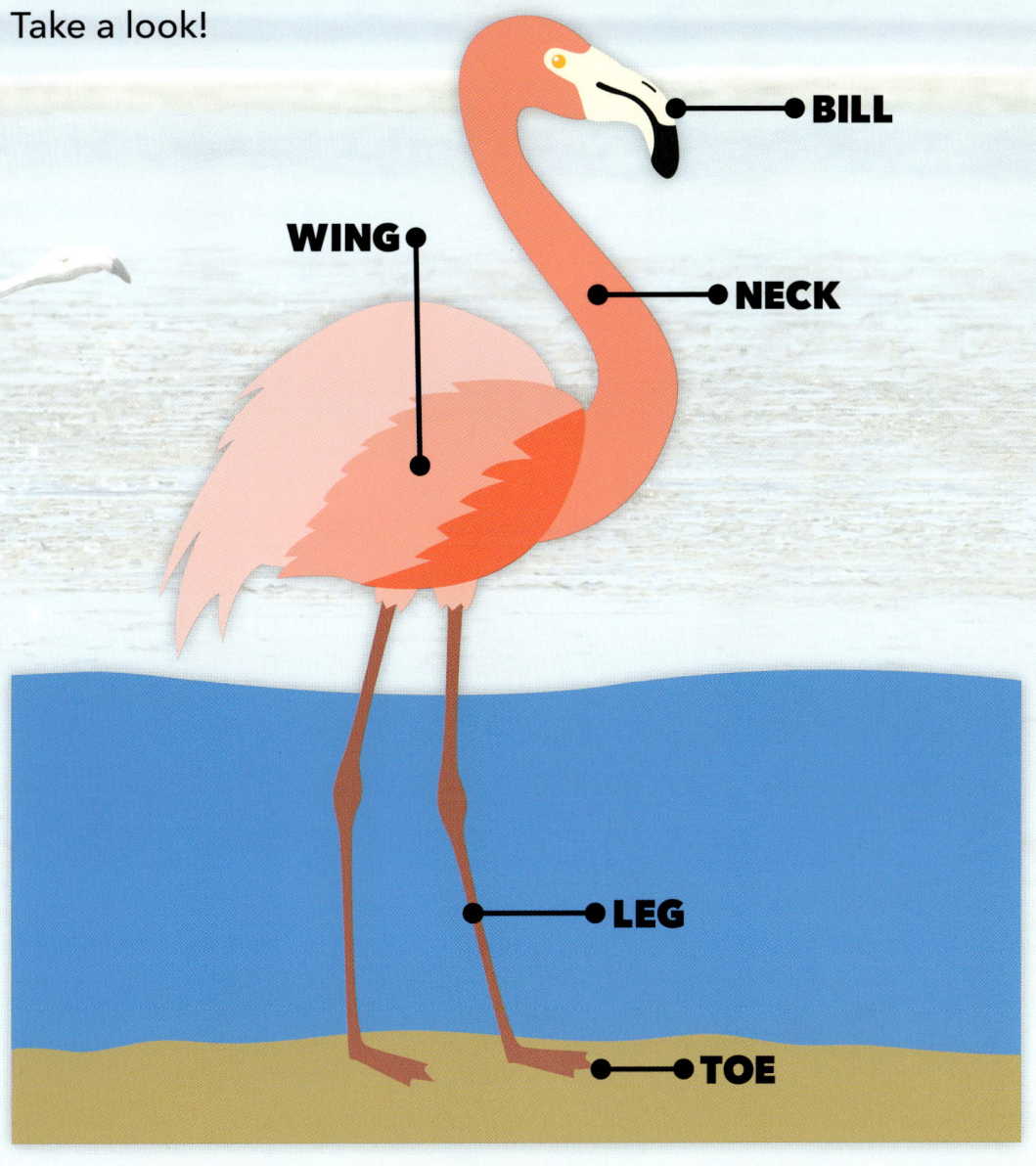

CHAPTER 1 9

CHAPTER 2
PINK FEATHERS

Flamingo flocks eat together, too. They live in large, shallow lakes or **lagoons**. Their favorite foods are found in them.

To eat, a flamingo holds its bill underwater. It sucks in water and food. Then it pumps the water out from the sides of its bill. The bill acts like a strainer. Water goes out, but food stays in. Yum!

bill

Crustaceans such as shrimp, crabs, and snails are in the water. **Algae** is, too. These all have large amounts of **pigments** called **carotenoids**. These are what give flamingos their pink color. The more of these the flamingos eat, the brighter their feathers.

DID YOU KNOW?

More than just a flamingo's feathers are pink. Its skin is pink. Even its blood is pink!

brine shrimp

CHAPTER 2 13

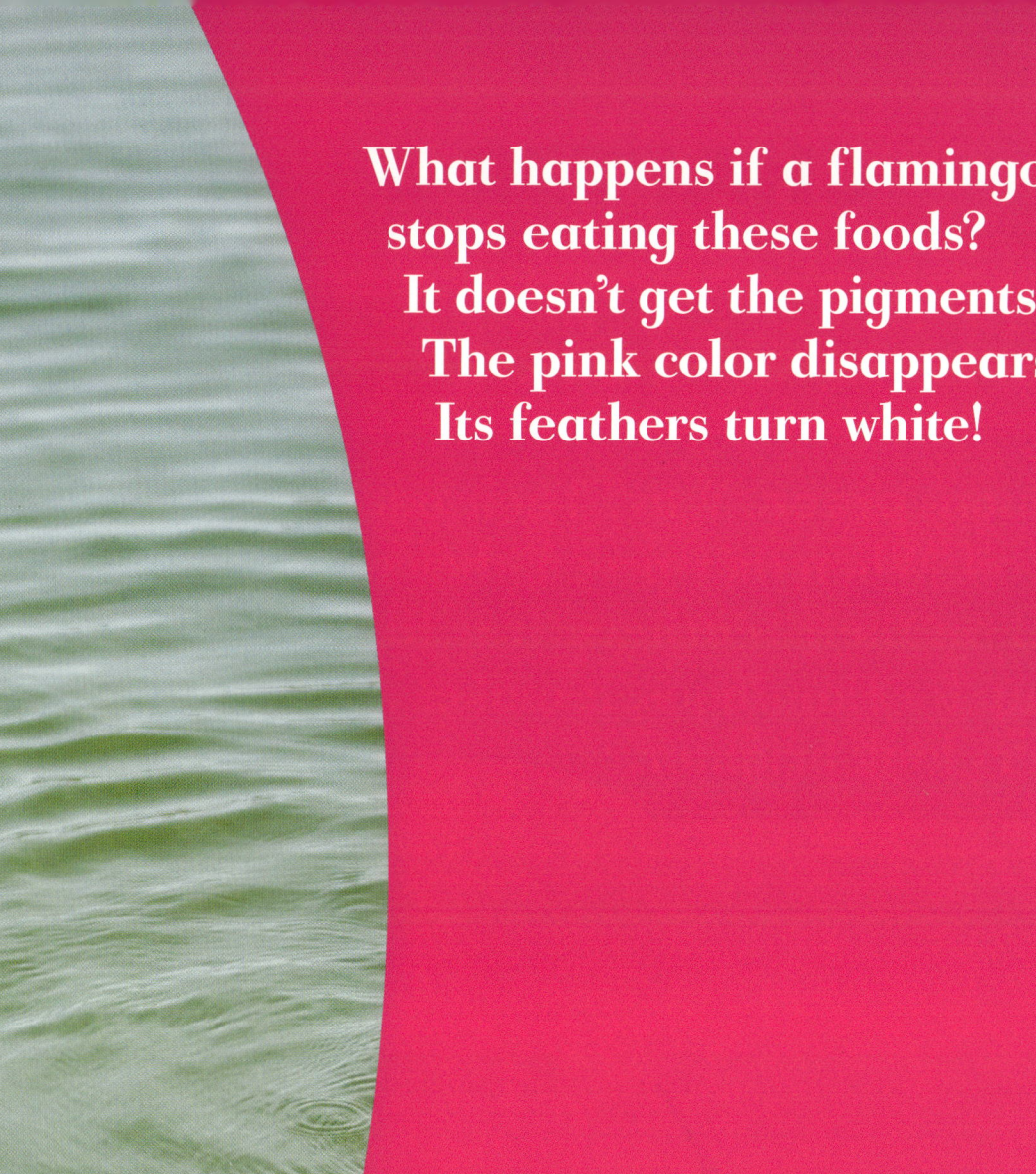

What happens if a flamingo stops eating these foods? It doesn't get the pigments. The pink color disappears. Its feathers turn white!

CHAPTER 2   15

CHAPTER 3
PINK DANCERS

Flamingos **preen**. Why? Their bodies make oil. When they preen, they wipe the oil on their feathers. It is like makeup for flamingos. It makes their feathers look brighter.

Bright pink feathers **attract** other flamingos. Why do the birds find this attractive? It shows that the bird is fit and good at finding food. This shows the other birds that it will be a good parent.

CHAPTER 3　17

Before choosing **mates**, the flock dances together. This shows off their coloring. Is another flamingo **impressed**? If so, the pair could mate.

CHAPTER 3 · 19

Flamingos usually lay just one egg each breeding season. The chick is born with gray or white feathers.

The chick won't turn pink until around age two. It will preen, dance, and show off its pink feathers, too!

DID YOU KNOW?

Both parents care for the chick. They feed it a special liquid called crop milk. Feeding drains the parents' feathers of color. They become white or pale pink!

CHAPTER 3 21

ACTIVITIES & TOOLS

TRY THIS!

COLOR-CHANGING FEATHERS

Flamingos' feathers change color based on what they eat. See how color can dye feathers or fabric with this activity!

What You Need:
- newspaper or an old kitchen towel
- white craft feathers, felt, or cotton fabric
- scissors
- pink or red foods, such as strawberries, raspberries, beets, or pieces of watermelon
- pink or red liquids, such as cranberry juice, pomegranate juice, or pink grapefruit juice
- pencil
- notebook

1. **Place some sheets of newspaper or an old kitchen towel onto the surface where you will be working.**

2. **If using felt or fabric, cut it into pieces about the size of a cell phone.**

3. **Rub or pour each food or liquid onto an individual feather or piece of fabric. Squish the berries a little before rubbing them onto the feather or fabric.**

4. **Which foods and liquids made the brightest shades of pink or red on your materials? Record your results in your notebook.**

GLOSSARY

algae: Small plants without roots or stems that grow mainly in water.

attract: To get something's interest.

carotenoids: Yellow or red pigments found widely in plants and animals.

continents: The seven large landmasses of Earth.

crustaceans: Sea creatures with outer skeletons.

energy: The ability or strength to do things without getting tired.

flocks: Groups of animals of one kind that live, travel, or feed together.

impressed: Felt admiration or respect.

lagoons: Shallow bodies of water that are separated from the sea by reefs.

mates: The male and female partners of a pair of animals.

pigments: Substances that give color to something.

preen: To clean and arrange feathers with the bill or beak.

webbing: Folds of skin that connect toes.

ACTIVITIES & TOOLS

INDEX

balance 6, 9
bill 9, 11
blood 12
carotenoids 12
chick 20
crop milk 20
crustaceans 12
dances 19, 20
eat 10, 11, 12, 15
egg 20
feathers 4, 12, 15, 16, 17, 20
flocks 5, 6, 10, 19
lagoons 10
lakes 10
leg 4, 6, 9
mates 19
necks 6, 9
oil 16
pigments 12, 15
pink 4, 12, 15, 17, 20
preen 16, 20
skin 12
sleep 4, 6
toes 8, 9
webbing 8, 9
white 15, 20

TO LEARN MORE

Finding more information is as easy as 1, 2, 3.
1. Go to www.factsurfer.com
2. Enter "flamingos" into the search box.
3. Click the "Surf" button to see a list of websites.

24 ACTIVITIES & TOOLS

1/2021   P   19
Birds
598.35
Kle

North Smithfield Public Library

P Birds 598.35 Kle
Klepeis, Alicia, 1971- author
Flamingos

35944001471422